Marie-Claire Di Carlo

I have a friend named Jesus

Marie-Claire Di Carlo

I have a friend named Jesus

And so do you

Blessed Hope Publishing

Imprint
Any brand names and product names mentioned in this book are subject to trademark, brand or patent protection and are trademarks or registered trademarks of their respective holders. The use of brand names, product names, common names, trade names, product descriptions etc. even without a particular marking in this work is in no way to be construed to mean that such names may be regarded as unrestricted in respect of trademark and brand protection legislation and could thus be used by anyone.

Cover image: www.ingimage.com

Publisher:
Blessed Hope Publishing
is a trademark of
International Book Market Service Ltd., member of OmniScriptum Publishing Group
17 Meldrum Street, Beau Bassin 71504, Mauritius

Printed at: see last page
ISBN: 978-613-7-88750-9

I have a friend named Jesus

Always believe, Jesus loves you. Here are some ways that Jesus loves us and shows He is our friend.

1-He listens to you

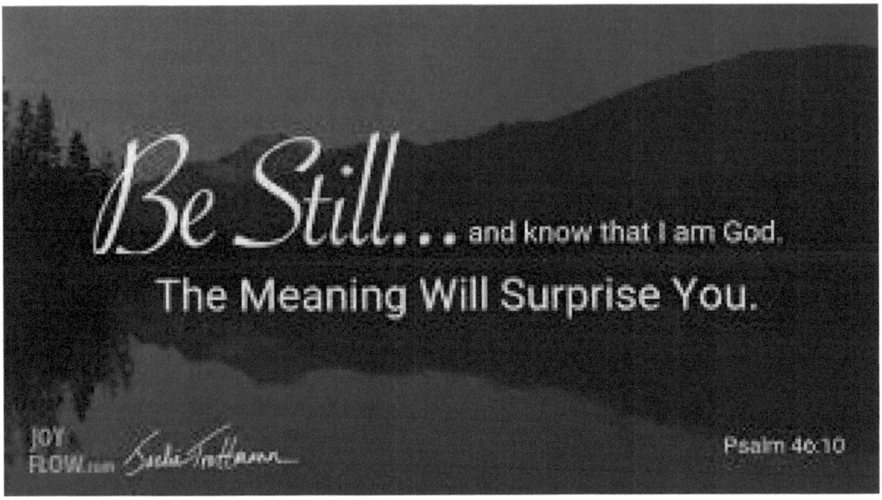
Be Still... and know that I am God.
The Meaning Will Surprise You.
JOY FLOW.com
Psalm 46:10

The best friend anyone can have is Jesus. He is silent and listens to ALL that you have to say and never replies back. Just dump your baggage on Jesus, let Him know how you feel. Let him fix your problems.

2-He eases our anxieties

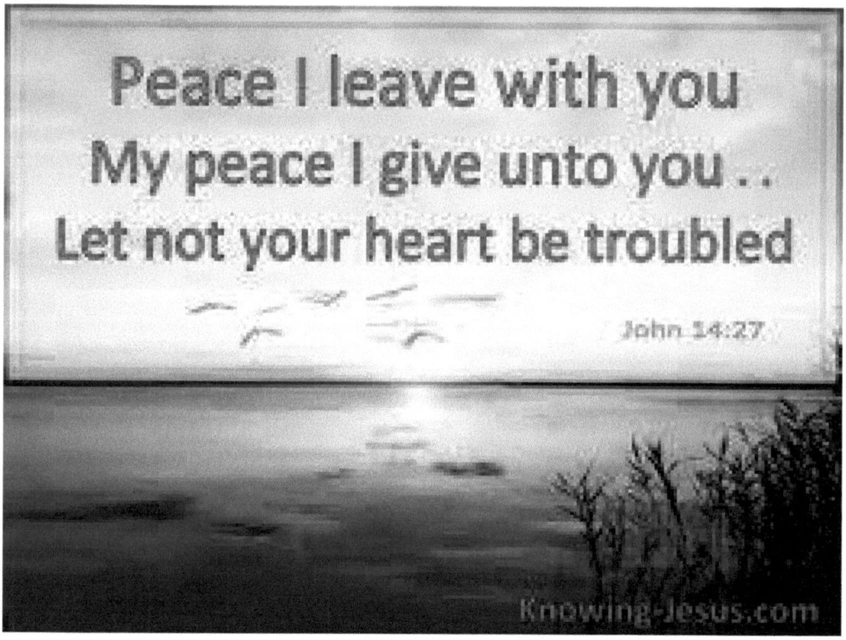
Peace I leave with you
My peace I give unto you . .
Let not your heart be troubled
John 14:27
Knowing-Jesus.com

Jesus knows us. And can calm our worries in an instant. Like the way He calmed the storm He can ease our emotions to Eternal Peace. Just ask Him too and He'll give you the strength and confidence that you need.

3-He loves everyone

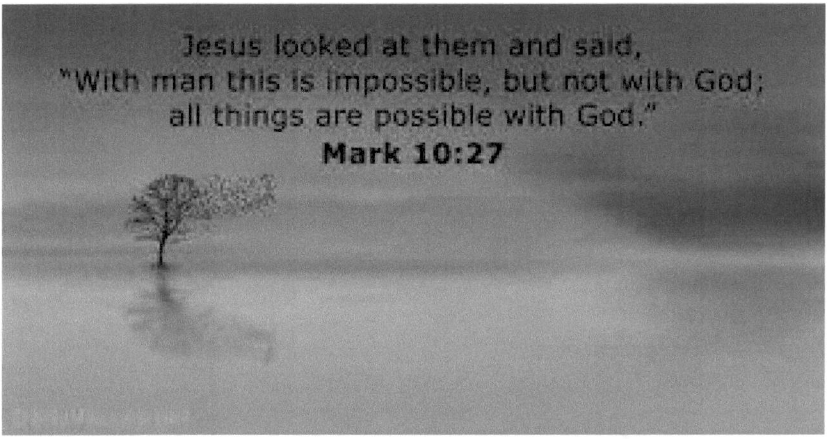
Jesus looked at them and said,
"With man this is impossible, but not with God;
all things are possible with God."
Mark 10:27

Jesus loves everyone, no discrimination. That's why He is God. He is not racist He loves us all and just wants us back in Heaven with his Father God.

4-He’s present in our prayers

WHEN DARKNESS IS SCREAMING
THAT GOD HAS ABANDONED YOU,
LISTEN TO THE CALM YET POWERFUL
VOICE OF JESUS SAYING,
"I WILL NEVER LEAVE YOU."

Everytime you call His name He is present. In our prayers, at work, in our sleep, just say His name and He is there with us. He loves us soo much. He wants our prayers to be heard and He sends them to the Father. Then God decides to grant it or not.

5-Jesus makes us behave good

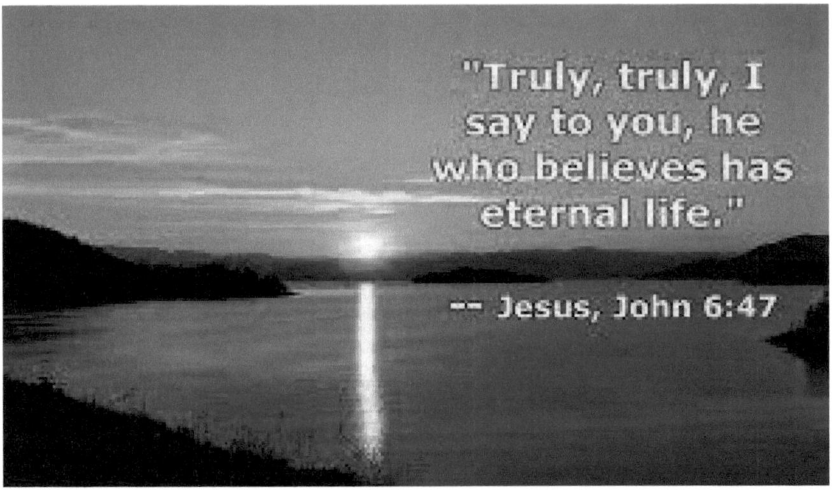
"Truly, truly, I say to you, he who believes has eternal life."
-- Jesus, John 6:47

We reflect our friends and when Jesus is your friend you become good. He is Eternally good and guides us to be like Him, like His Father.

6-He doesn’t judge. His judgement comes from the Almighty

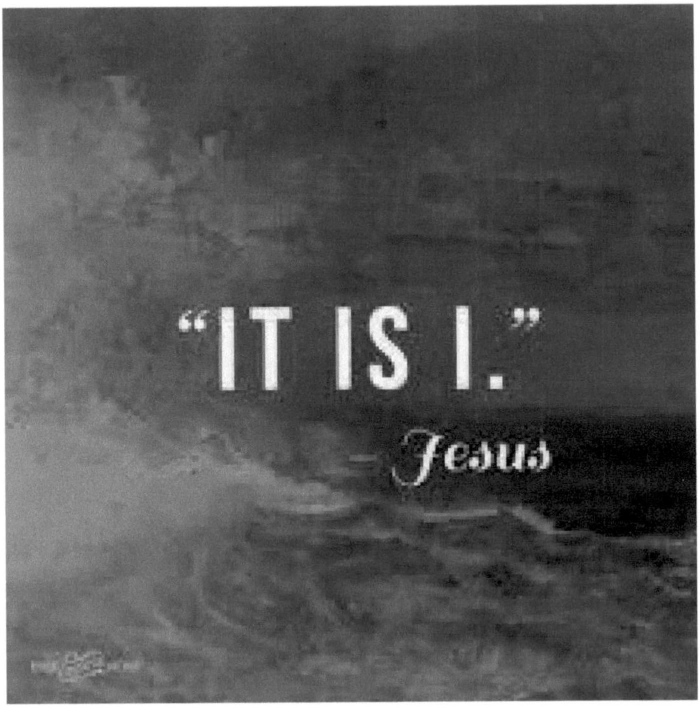
"IT IS I."
Jesus

Jesus told us that He doesn't judge us, but His Father does and tells Jesus who to judge. He loves us but the Final Judgement will pass at the end of time and God will tell Jesus to judge us and our lives.

7-He knows our thoughts and tries to calm them

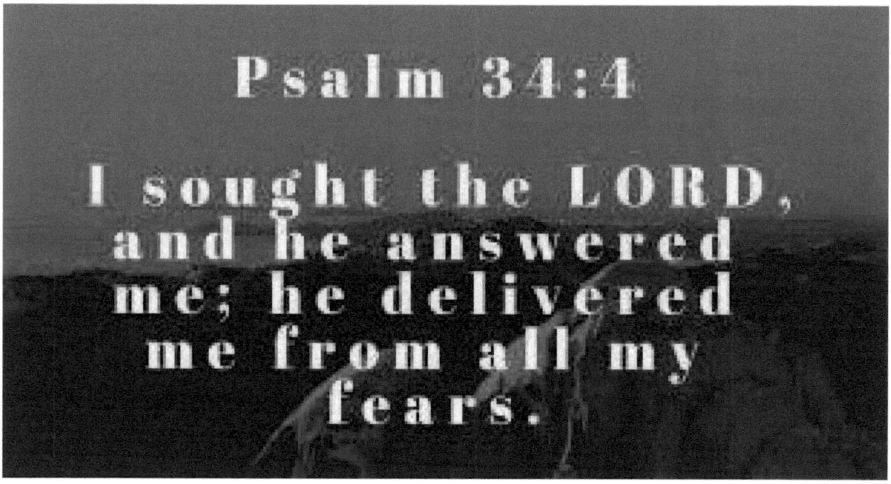
Psalm 34:4
I sought the LORD, and he answered me; he delivered me from all my fears.

Jesus is our friend because He knows our thoughts and tries to calm them when we are anxious. He knows our fears and is by our side in life guiding us and helping us through it. He is our bestfriend.

8-He is everywhere

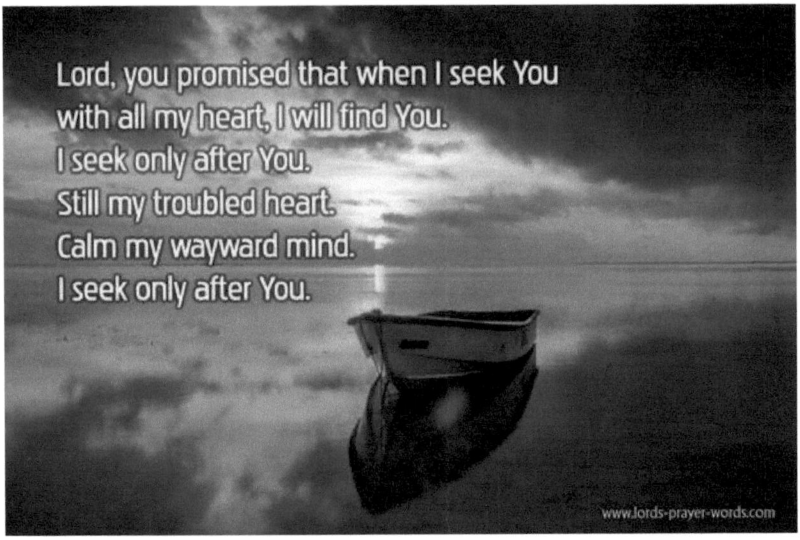
Lord, you promised that when I seek You
with all my heart, I will find You.
I seek only after You.
Still my troubled heart.
Calm my wayward mind.
I seek only after You.
www.lords-prayer-words.com

Travel often? Jesus is with you wherever you go. I remember when I was returning from the HolyLand I saw outside the airplane window Jesus' face in the sky. He truly is with you wherever you go. Never fear Jesus is here.

9-Going to church to find Him

Be not afraid,
only believe.
Mark 5:36

Truly to reconnect with Jesus and His father you must go to His house, in other words church. Jesus' body is there in the Eucharist and He then enters our bodies to purify them. Don't have anyone to go to church with? Jesus is your friend and He will be there.

10-Whenever you feel alone, you're not alone

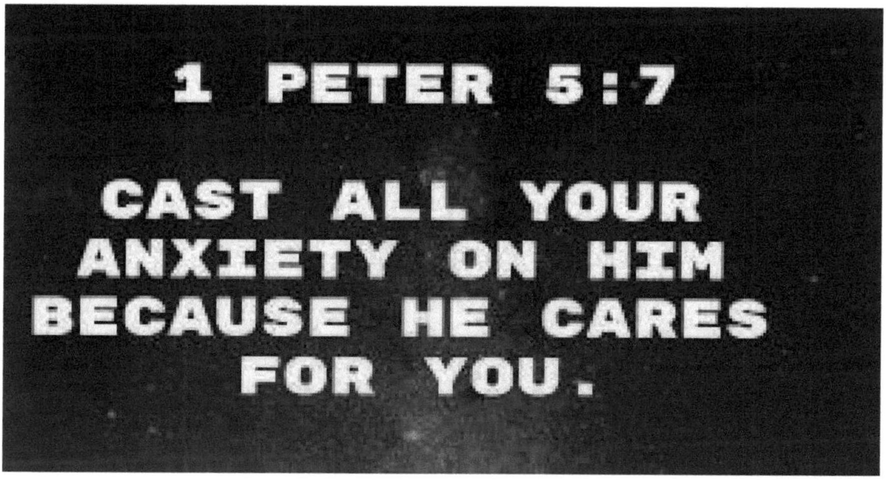
1 PETER 5:7
CAST ALL YOUR
ANXIETY ON HIM
BECAUSE HE CARES
FOR YOU.

You are never alone, Jesus said He'd never leave us. I believe that. When you feel lonely, imagine Jesus is there. Don't just imagine it, believe it! He is our friend, who happens to be a King too and He never leaves our side. He cares about us.

11- He is like having a superhero as a friend.

Give
THANKS
to the
LORD
for
HE is
GOOD.
His LOVE
ENDURES forever
PSALM 136:1

He can make miracles, He can rise from the dead, He is better than a superhero, and to top it off He is your friend. It's good to have friends but Jesus most importantly will always be by your side, through good and bad. Thank you Jesus.

MIX
Papier aus verantwortungsvollen Quellen
Paper from responsible sources
FSC® C105338

Printed by Books on Demand GmbH, Norderstedt / Germany